Comments from Readers:

"A Month of Sundays is a soul-inspiring c_____ Divinity. I love the reflections at the end of the chapters, and I am inspired to go deeper into my relationship with Love in every chapter."

"I am happy and grateful when you remind me that Peace in my life expands each time I act on my commitment to Peace."

Malia Brown,
Executive Life Coach
Creator of Peace Amplified

"A Month of Sundays is a book that is consciously designed to bring you closer to God. When one reads the Message, answers the Questions and Journal his own thoughts, one can only find complete freedom in his Spirit."

Artelle Gandy,
Prosperity Consciousness, LLC
Founder

"I think this will be a true blessing to the body of Christ. What I saw blessed me. This entry stood out for me, 'In this Holy Moment, I Can Begin Again   Almighty Love Empowers Me to Persevere.' "

Allennita Cooks,
Educator/Author
The Grandfather Tree

"Each Sunday morning, I select one of the mini-Sabbath experiences in your book to focus on. I have found this to be a wonderful way to take in and reflect upon each of the messages that you provide us in this blessing. This practice serves to remind me of God's love, presence, assurance, and grace always available to me. Thank you, dear friend, for the breadth and depth of your thoughts and insights that you so freely share."

Mary L. Horton,
MH and Associates, Consulting
Prinicpal Consultant

A Month

of

Sundays

Practicing Sabbath
Every Day

Charles W. Thomas, Jr.

For information about this title or to order other books and/or electronic media, contact the publisher:
web site http://www.amonthofsundays.us

ISBN 978-1-7328026-0-5

Printed in the United States of America
Cover design: Judi Paliungas, PalimorDesignStudios.com
Interior design: A Book Writer's Midwife – Anne Perrah & John Lunsford

Publisher's Cataloging-In-Publication Data
(Prepared by The Donohue Group, Inc.)
Names: Charles W. Thomas, Jr.
Title: A Month of Sundays: Practicing Sabbath Every Day.
Identifiers: ISBN 978-1-7328026-0-5

Dedication

To My Parents

Johnnie C. Thomas

And

Charles W. Thomas, Sr.

Author's Note:

My prayer for you is that this book becomes a reminder of your companionship with your inner Divinity. I pray that you experience an abundance of life that fulfills the mission of Christ on earth, to have life and to have it abundantly.

The premise of this book is to demonstrate the efficacy of having a daily spiritual practice. As a member of the laity and an heir to Christian faith and practice, I find it ironic that to have a 'daily sabbath' practice is a type of oxymoron. In the most common usage I have found, Sabbath practice is the setting aside a one day in seven to rest and commune with God. The 'Month of Sundays' idea is to create a mini-Sabbath experience every day regardless of the day of a weekly Sabbath you currently observe.

To that end I will share several intentions that may help you connect with the spirit of the book.

1. The questions associated with the messages are designed to encourage you to discover something new in your thinking or to clarify an old belief.
2. Some of the messages you will read are reflective affirmations which implicitly invite you to confirm your life-enhancing assumptions and to release your constrictive assumptions.
3. Use the 'My Thoughts' page to write your own affirmations or examine your thoughts and feelings relative to the message.
4. In some of the messages I am sharing a personal experience or point of view. Read those messages as though a brother or close friend is inviting you into reflection and prayer
5. Some messages are introduced as 'A Message from Immanuel.' These messages are inspired by Scripture, prayer or meditation. Use the 'Self-Reflective Questions' and 'My Thought' space to examine your intellectual and emotional response.

Dear
Linda and Roy,
Thank you for your
support. May you
be Opulently Blessed,
Charles

May your experience of A Month of Sundays,
surprise, heal, delight and bless you in ways
that deepen your awareness of the Divine!

— *Charles*

Table of Contents

Acknowledgments

I wish to acknowledge Dr. Anne Perrah and John Lunsford, the book writer's mid-wife team for their caring support in the delivery of this book. Judi Paliungas my talented and patient cover designer. Mary Morrissey my mentor and friend who is responsible for the resource-rich community in which the book gestated. Rai Jordan, Visioning Coach and friend for helping to clarify the highest vision of the message, My Master Coach and friend, Kirsten Welles whose contagious brave thinking helped me jettison the paradigms that were constricting the birth of the publication. Dr. Bobbie Brooks, my first teacher in metaphysics, My prayer partners, Mrs. Allennita Cooks, friend, writer and partner in seeking and sharing God's Love via the written word. Malia Brown, my partner in believing opulently, Rev. E. J. Joier, Rev. Gregory Guice, Pastor and Senior Minister of Detroit Unity Temple, Mary Horton, Pamela McKiever, Novlett Ellis, David Joseph, Cindy Yamamoto Master Mind Partner, Rabbi Dorit Edut, Artelle Gandy and Tonya Brown and all the members of JoiHaven prayer ministry, the Detroit Unity Temple Prayer Chaplains, The DUT Forgiveness Ministry and Forgiveness Advocates. Dianne Rhodes who edited the first draft of this material 5 years before it reached its current state. My Loving daughters Cadrinia, Carla and Kristin. My loving and infinitely patient wife LaVonne and everyone at Detroit Unity Temple who listened to the Dial-A-Thought calls, especially those who encouraged me to "do something" with the messages I shared. Please forgive me. I know I have not named everyone who has contributed to the release of A Month of Sundays, Practicing the Sabbath Every Day. I'm sorry, please forgive me, thank you. I love you.

To see a World in a Grain of Sand
And a Heaven in a Wild Flower,
Hold Infinity in the palm of your hand
And Eternity in an hour.

– William Blake
(from "Auguries of Innocence")

A Message from Immanuel: Peace in Faith

I open my heart and my mind to Immanuel, God with me.

"For I know the thoughts that I think toward you, says the Lord, thoughts of peace and not of evil, to give you a future and a hope." - Jeremiah 29:11

Beloved friend and companion, the thoughts I think toward you are peaceful. I Love you as I Am Loved; as I love Myself, I love you. I Am Faithful to you. I Am here to familiarize you with My presence and to support you in strengthening your faith in Our Father, Love-Self-Evident, I AM. Trust in the Father is our assurance that All Is Well. When we know the Oneness WE ARE, the Truth I AM is manifest. The truth born of sight and hearing alone is minuscule in comparison with the Truth I AM.

Listen to Me, share with Me, ask Me what you will. Follow Me and allow our Father to anoint you with the Wisdom of Peace and the peace of wisdom. Then you can know, beyond mere human understanding, that We are One with Our Father.

Let us Pray:

I invite you to pray and meditate on the following scriptures –

"Therefore the Lord himself will give you a sign. Behold, the virgin will conceive, and bear a son, and shall call his name Immanuel." - Isaiah 7:14

"Peace I leave with you, My peace I give to you; not as the world gives do I give to you. Let not your heart be troubled, neither let it be afraid."
- John 14:27

Self-Reflection Questions

Question 1: What is being revealed during this time of prayer and meditation?

_____

_____

_____

_____

_____

_____

Question 2: What is your experience of being One with God?

_____

_____

_____

_____

_____

_____

_____

My Thoughts

A Sabbath In Every Day

Today and every day, I remember the Sabbath and keep it holy.

"And he said unto them, The Sabbath was made for man, and not man for the Sabbath"
- Mark 2:27

Usually, we think of the Sabbath as being a specific day of the week which we reserve for worshiping and honoring God. Today, however, let us look at Sabbath as a state of mind or mental attainment which we can achieve at any time. Sabbath is a state of surrender to God's Peace and Comfort, where we cease all activity, even the commotion of our restless conscious thinking. Today take time to stop all personal effort and allow the Holy Spirit to work in your mind, your heart and your affairs. This is the day the Lord has made, so let us rest and enjoy delicious, intimate contact with God. Each day let us establish a time to practice Sabbath, and each week set aside a day in which we prioritize God. During these sacred moments and days, we feel and know, that the Father, living within us, is irresistibly orchestrating everyone and everything to work together peacefully and harmoniously for our individual and collective well-being.

Let Us Pray:

Dearest Lord, I now surrender my all to you in this holy time of Sabbath. I open my mind and heart to Your Presence. Speak Love to me. Open my eyes to that which You would have me see. Let me see and know You. Teach me to discern Your many expressions. Cleanse my ears so that I may hear Your Truth wherever It is spoken. Let me hear Your intention in the speech of all who address me. Every day, Lord, I choose to be still and wait patiently for the awareness that You and I are One, I AM that, I am. I am endowed with the wisdom, patience, and the consistency to honor a daily and weekly Sabbath. I now let go of anxiety, worry, and urgency. I rest in Perfect Peace which restores my soul.

Thank God, for answering prayer!
Selah!
So It Is!
Amen!

"He makes me lie down in green pastures. He leads me beside still waters. He restores my soul. He guides me in the paths of righteousness for his name's sake."
- Psalms 23:2-3 (NKJV)

"And we know that all things work together for good to them that love God, to them who are the called according to his purpose."
- Romans 8:28 (KJV)

Self-Reflection Questions

Question 1: What can you imagine doing to add variety to your daily Sabbath practice?

_____

_____

_____

_____

_____

_____

Question 2: This week what will you do to prioritize God, at least for a day?

_____

_____

_____

_____

_____

_____

_____

My Thoughts

A Peaceful Soul
Has a Core Value of Peace

I value peace, I affirm peace
and I am peaceful.

"And he arose, and rebuked the wind, and said unto the sea, Peace, be still. And the wind ceased, and there was a great calm." - Mark 4:39 KJV

When my soul is at peace, I am inclined to be calm and aware of my surroundings with uncommon clarity. Few things can rattle my sense of contentment, so when something does tug me away from my peaceful center, I am alerted to pay attention to it.

A mindset or way of thinking that is not aligned with the Truth of peace causes my perception of conflict and a need to attack or get even. I am grateful when I notice the shifts in thinking that alert me to the unexamined habits that disturb my peace. When I notice an unwanted pattern, I have the opportunity to choose a more appropriate response and reestablish my calm mindset. It is easier to remain peaceful in adversity when I allow the Divine Presence in me to remind me of my commitment to peace.

The Holy Spirit, active in me, is stronger than any outside forces. My mind is more open to unexpected answers when I am peacefully centered in my soul.

Let Us Pray:

Thank You God for the Peace that surpasses human understanding. The Peace of Your Holy Presence inside of me and surrounding me is my assurance of peace in my life. I am grateful that at the end of today, I will have lived another day blessed with peace and harmony. There is a blessing to be found in everything when I think positively and allow peace to reign in my life. I am happy and grateful when You remind me that Peace in my life expands each time I act on my commitment to peace.

Thank, You God!
I am at Peace!
Selah!

"Peace I leave with you. My peace I give to you; not as the world gives, give I to you. Don't let your heart be troubled, neither let it be fearful."
- John 14:27 (WEB)

Self-Reflection Questions

Question 1: What is the level of your commitment to living a peace-filled life?

_____

_____

_____

_____

_____

_____

Question 2: What can you do now to experience more peace today?

_____

_____

_____

_____

_____

_____

_____

My Thoughts

God Is Our Sufficiency!

I am blessed with sufficiency.

"For the LORD your God is he that goeth with you, to fight for you against your enemies, to save you."
- Deuteronomy 20:4 KJV

God is more than enough. Omnipotence defies human understanding. In this time of thoughtful consideration and prayer let's open ourselves to the embrace of Omnipotent Sufficiency. Imagine that we are blessing the people within our spheres of influence beyond their familiar expectations. We give thanks for their evolving relationship with All-Sufficiency. As we become more aware of the flow of God's Love flowing through us, we imagine It flowing through them as well. God is sufficient in all circumstances, interactions and endeavors.

Let Us Pray:

Dear Lord of Provision, I am grateful for Your rich and generous blessings, material and non-material. I am confident that there is always enough. Even as you fed the people in the wilderness, You feed my Soul, nourish my body and renew my mind. Thank You, God for supplying the needs of the people within the influence of my prayers. I appreciate their blessings as much as mine. I am filled with joy as I realize how perfectly God is blessing everyone with whom I interact.

Thank You God!
Amen!

"Haven't I commanded you? Be strong and of good courage; don't be afraid, neither be dismayed: for the Lord your God is with you wherever you go."
- Joshua 1:9

Self-Reflection Questions

Question 1: How do you see yourself in the flow of substance and blessings?

_____

_____

_____

_____

_____

_____

Question 2: As you imagine yourself an instrument of All-Sufficiency, how do you see yourself behaving?

_____

_____

_____

_____

_____

_____

_____

My Thoughts

God is My Role Model
for Generosity

I am generous.

"But this I say: He who sows sparingly will also reap sparingly, and he who sows bountifully will also reap bountifully."
- 2 Corinthians 9:6

I believe that to be generous is to give freely to others in a variety of ways. My generosity brings joy to my heart. I feel good when I help people in need or to show friends and loved ones that I appreciate them. Being generous is now a part of my gratefulness for my blessings of provision and abundance.

Sharing my time with others and offering a smile to the people I meet are simple ways that I share my joy and nurture my generosity. Consciously sharing my time is like giving a bit of myself to another person. I think of it as an act of love; it is my way of attempting to love as Christ Loves.

Giving to others brings me a satisfying joy. I donate my formerly used clothing, appliances and other items to organizations that are making a difference in my community. I love being generous. Giving helps me feel opulent, as I experience the flow of Good in circulation.

Let Us Pray:

Dear Father of Generosity, Your very nature is Love! Your Love is generously given to all who would receive it. Help me to love in like manner, especially in matters of forgiveness. Father, I seek to be generously compassionate and understanding. Today, I choose to be generous with everyone I contact. When I am generous, I generate the kindness, caring, and sharing I would like to receive. I find that the more generous I become, the more I feel fulfilled. What acts of generosity would You have me perform today, Lord?

*I am open and receptive to Your guidance,
and I am ready to give!
Thank You God!*

"Give, and it will be given to you: good measure, pressed down, shaken together, and running over will be put into your bosom. For with the same measure that you use, it will be measured back to you."
- Luke 6:38 NKJV

Self-Reflection Questions

Question 1: What acts of generosity bring you joy?

_____

_____

_____

_____

_____

_____

Question 2: What is the relationship of generosity to prosperity?

_____

_____

_____

_____

_____

_____

_____

My Thoughts

Praying the Love That Is God

I form my prayers in Love
to fulfill God's Will.

"You shall love the Lord your God with all your heart, and with all your soul, and with all your might."—Deuteronomy 6:5 (NASB)

Any time is the right time to pray—at the beginning of the day, just before a meal, during a worship service, and at this moment!

There is a lot written about prayer. There are many approaches to prayer. There are sophisticated experiments performed to test the impact of prayer. At this moment, let's think less about how we appeal to Love and turn our attention to the experience of Almighty Love. Savor, Its indwelling and surrounding Presence. Endeavor to sense Love's Presence, feel It, listen for It, intuit It. Invoke It, evoke It and just KNOW Love is present - now!

Let Us Pray:

Dear God, I love You with all my heart, with all my soul, and with all my might. Teach me to express my love and gratitude for Your vitalizing Presence as Life expressing abundantly throughout creation. I am grateful for the assurance of Your Wisdom. Divine Wisdom influences every thought that takes form in my awareness.

Father, how may I demonstrate my love today? I have the notion that as I love others I am expressing my love for You. In quiet, reflective prayer I experience the serenity of the Silence. In affirmative prayer, I speak the truth with conviction, building a strong foundation of faith and gratitude for Your power and presence.

When I authentically love the I Am that I Am, I am actually loving You. I open my mind and my heart to more Love, more of Your Presence, more Light, and more Compassion. I welcome the expanding possibilities which are indicative of Your Presence with me. Encourage me, that is, give me the courage to love those whom I am reluctant to love. Jesus is my role model for Love. Ignite the Christ Mind and the sacred heart of Jesus in me to show me Love in action as the I AM; I am, doing what is mine to do today.

Thank You, God! Amen!

"A new commandment I give to you, that you love one another, even as I have loved you, that you also love one another. By this all men will know that you are My disciples, if you have love for one another."
- John 13:34-35 (NASB)

Self-Reflection Questions

Question 1: How is loving your neighbor like loving God?

_____

_____

_____

_____

_____

_____

Question 2: How comfortable are you using the words God and Love interchangeably?

_____

_____

_____

_____

_____

_____

_____

My Thoughts

I Am Blessed, and I Endeavor to Be a Blessing

I bless my sphere of influence and all contained therein.

"And let the peace of God rule in your hearts, to which also you were called in one body; and be thankful." - Colossians 3:15

Today, I revel in my expanding and deepening relationship with God and I bless my Sphere of Influence. All of us have a field of influence. It is an energy field in which we impact people, conditions, and probabilities beyond our current understanding. Infants have a comparatively small but growing area of influence, individuals taking their last breath have an influence field and so it is for everyone regardless of age or station in life. Lately, I have been giving more attention to my impact on the world around me. I would love to see the results of my impact reflect the activity of the Holy Spirit. I imagine my influence existing in the form of a multidimensional sphere, having a spiritual nature, existing in multiple dimensions and creating ripple effects I do not yet understand. Within this sphere, I am affected by the reciprocating influences of my intentions to bless and to be a blessing.

Let Us Pray:

Thank You, God, for blessing all of us with an awareness of our individual and collective spheres of influence. As we expand our awareness and our capacities to love and share the best of who we are and what we have, bless everyone and everything within our spheres of influence. Thank You for the realization that everyone and everything within our Influence, influences us in proportion to the quality and intensity of the energy we project. Therefore, may the power of our influence always have a high vibration of Love! May our way-of-being consistently serve Freedom! May our influence confer and preserve Peace! May our intentions intensify Light and dispel shadow! May our prayers promote healing and honor Life! May our conversations serve Opulence, Beauty and Unity! Thank You, God for blessing and expanding our Spheres of Influence to include this planet and all Your Creation!

Thank You God!
We are complete!
Selah!

"Jesus said to him, 'You shall love the Lord your God with all your heart, with all your soul, and with all your mind.' This is the first and great commandment. And the second is like it: 'You shall love your neighbor as yourself.' On these two commandments hang all the Law and the Prophets."
Matthew 22:37-40

Self-Reflection Questions

Question 1: How do you imagine blessing everyone and everything in your Sphere of Influence today?

_____

_____

_____

_____

_____

_____

Question 2: Who and what do you consider to be within your Sphere of Influence?

_____

_____

_____

_____

_____

_____

_____

My Thoughts

Oneness of Life

Today I celebrate
my oneness with Life.

"Confess your offenses to one another, and pray one for another, that you may be healed. The insistent prayer of a righteous person is powerfully effective."
- James 5:16

It has been said that prayer is the highest form of mind action. Today let us pray from a personal, local, global and even universal perspective. We can pray for ourselves, giving thanks for our health, well-being and prosperity. We can give thanks for harmonious and healed relationships. We can accept God's abundance with prayerful gratitude. Let us expand the reach of our "prayer net" to include our loved ones, friends, acquaintances and strangers alike, giving thanks for their healing, prosperity and peace of mind. We now expand the reach of our prayers to encompass the entire earth and everything that is in it. Let's now shine the Light of our Being on the planet, so that we clearly see it sustainable, life-supporting, alive and very good, just as God made it.

Let Us Pray:

Thank You God for inspiring me in this holy moment to offer a prayer of thanksgiving for Life. I am learning to spontaneously express Your Wisdom and Truth within the infinitude of the present moment, Lord. In doing so, I bless everyone within my sphere of influence. Thank You God for the gift of prayer, the privileged communication between You and me, which results in my deepening understanding that You and I are One and that I am one with the rest of humanity. Thank You for blessing all of Your creation with Life and with interconnectedness and mutual support. I am blessed by the loving support of plants, animals and the entire Matrix of Life which comprises Planet Earth. I therefore bless all life on earth, from the gigantic creatures of the ocean to the smallest microbes that make all other life possible. Give me the wisdom, understanding and compassion to see the whole of Life in its composite grandeur and to gratefully appreciate the beauty and importance of each individual component. I thank You God for the capacity to bless, heal and prosper the earth and everyone and everything in it.

In Jesus' Name!
It Is So!
Amen!

"And God saw everything that he had made, and, behold, it was very good..."
- Genesis 1:31

Self-Reflection Questions

Question 1: In what ways can you imagine extending your 'prayer net'?

_____

_____

_____

_____

_____

_____

Question 2: As you pray, when do you know your prayer has been answered?

_____

_____

_____

_____

_____

_____

_____

My Thoughts

The Christ in Me Recognizes the Christ In You

I behold the Christ in you!

Therefore if anyone is in Christ, he is a new creation. The old things have passed away. Behold, all things have become new.
- 2 Corinthians 5:17

Today, let's look for the best in everyone we encounter or think about. Let's start with ourselves. What do you appreciate about yourself today? Do you acknowledge how well your body serves you? Regardless of aches, pains or anything else that may be going on in your body, listen for a message of hope and possibility. Christ in you is a healing Presence. Do you appreciate that you have come a long way in life, surviving storms, disappointments, tough decisions and challenging relationships? Your powers to overcome, heal, recover, prosper, encourage others and to live to the best of your ability are just a portion of the Inner Christ. Today, see if you can find evidence of these abilities or other virtues in the people you meet, especially those who don't interest you, who annoy you or who appear to have nothing in common with you. Ask God to be revealed to you, wherever you go and in all circumstances today.

Let Us Pray:

Dear Lord, I thank You for this day. I appreciate today's blessings, adventures, revelations and breakthroughs. I value its successes and its failures. This is a glorious day and I rejoice in it. Father, show me the Christ in everyone I meet or think about today. I would be delighted if I could discern some redeeming value or hidden beauty in every person who crosses my mind or crosses my path today. I see You so clearly in some people and I forget to even look for You in others. I am ready to give that up and I am willing to behold Christ in everyone, including those who would deny that Christ exists. Shine Your Light of Understanding on my ignorance and Your Light of Love on my intolerance and misjudgment. You are active within me as the energy of my motivation, inspiration, perception, enlightenment and Love. I believe You are present in others, just as You are present within me. You energize them in similar yet diverse ways. Reveal Yourself in others to me today so that I can know others as You know me.

Thank You God!
All Is Well!
Selah!

"I am the vine. You are the branches. He who remains in me, and I in him, the same bears much fruit, for apart from me you can do nothing."
- John 15:5

Self-Reflection Questions

Question 1: How would you describe your Inner-Presence of Love?

_____

_____

_____

_____

_____

_____

_____

Question 2: Who represents Love's Presence in your life?

_____

_____

_____

_____

_____

_____

_____

_____

My Thoughts

I Allow the Divine to Produce New Conditions in My Life

My mind is a center of Divine Operation.

"And we know that all things work together for good to those who love God, to those who are the called according to His purpose." – Romans 8:28

Today, as I was considering how to establish more order in my physical environment, I remembered how Genevieve Behrend brought a new order into her financial affairs by internalizing one of Thomas Troward's ideas about Divine Operation. You can learn more from her book, *Your Invisible Power*.

She writes that Troward's idea seemed to be the greatest thing she had ever read. The following words arrested her attention to the degree that she committed them to memory, and repeated them several times a day until she crossed a threshold of understanding which ultimately transformed her life.

"My mind is a center of Divine operation. The Divine operation is always for expansion and fuller expression, and this means the production of something beyond what has gone before, something entirely new, not included in the past experience, though proceeding out of it by an orderly sequence of growth. Therefore, since the Divine cannot change its inherent nature, It must operate in the same manner with me; consequently, in my own special world, of which I am the center, It will move forward to produce new conditions, always in advance of any that have gone before."

Let Us Pray:

Dear Lord, help me to know myself as an integral part of the Divine Order You Are. I open myself to Your Divine operation in my mind. Thank, You for supporting me in my intention to have a deeper and more intimate relationship with Divine Order. Thank You for this experience of deepening faith in Your Invisible Presence. I welcome the anointing of my thinking process and the ordering of my thoughts and feelings which keep me focused on Your Holy Purpose regarding my life. Regardless of outer appearances, I surrender to the Divine Operation within me that gives rise to the visible forms of order that bless my life. Father, I am grateful for my increasing capacity to see Order in the face of disorder. Thank You for establishing useful forms and structures of order that bless everyone and everything within my field of influence. I am happy and grateful to feel and know the blessing of Divine Order!

Thank You, God!
Amen!

"Let all things be done decently and in order. For God is a God not of disorder but of peace."
- 1 Corinthians 14:40 & 33

Self-Reflection Questions

Question 1: What can you do to cultivate your mind as a center of expansion and increase?

_____

_____

_____

_____

_____

_____

Question 2: Imagine that you have assimilated the idea of your mind being a center of Divine Operation, what new condition or circumstance would you love to invite into your life?

_____

_____

_____

_____

_____

_____

My Thoughts

Surrender to Love, Embody Peace and Prosper

God is Love; I embody peace.

"He who pursues righteousness and love finds life, prosperity and honor."
– Proverbs 21:21

Today, let's contemplate Love, Peace and Prosperity. Can you imagine them to be fundamental desires of your soul? What images come to mind? You can experience Love without being able to define it or even describe it; we know It when It is present. It is Divine! Choose peace, right now in this holy moment, just set the intention to feel peaceful. Let go of every thought, idea or impulse that tries to steal your peace. As you relax into the peacefulness of Love's Presence, you are experiencing prosperity at its Source, formless, powerful and overflowing with possibility. If you are finding this difficult or feel it is impossible, remember that with God all things are possible.

Let Us Pray:

Dear Lord, on this holy day, let me experience You as Love. Let me find peace in my heart and help me to know this as my true prosperity. In Your Word, You reveal Jerusalem as the habitation of peace. Create in me, Lord, a new Jerusalem where I can find the peace within, the calm center for which my soul yearns. Within this inner place of peace, I surrender to Love, I surrender to You. I choose to embody peace through my surrender. I still my mind and relax. I am grateful! I love my life and I prosper. Thank You God!

I Surrender!
I Let It Be!
I Let God!
I Let Go!
I Am!
Amen!

Pray for the Peace of the New Jerusalem:
"May those who love you be secure. May there be peace within your walls and security within your citadels."
For the sake of my brothers and friends, I will say, "Peace be within you."
For the sake of the house of the LORD our God, I will seek your prosperity.
— Psalms 122:6-9

Self-Reflection Questions

Question 1: What images come into your mind as you think about Love, Peace and Prosperity?

_____

_____

_____

_____

_____

_____

Question 2: What recurring thought or belief steals or kills your experience of peace?

_____

_____

_____

_____

_____

_____

_____

My Thoughts

My Best Blessing Is to Bless Another

Blessings follow me wherever I go.

"Surely goodness and mercy shall follow me all the days of my life: and I will dwell in the house of the LORD forever."
- Psalms 23:6

Today my friend, join me in the contemplation of the following statements:

In all things, I am blessed and I make it a point to take notice of all the good in my life. Even if I experience challenging events, I strive to remember how blessed I am.

I always have what I need. And often, I have more than enough. I am loved abundantly and I eagerly love in return.

Infinite resources are at my fingertips. In the realm of supply, including money, I always have enough to cover my needs and to meet the desires of my heart.

If I experience times when I feel lack, I remind myself that, in truth, I have all that I require. Whether I am employed or unemployed, partnered or single, with others or alone, I feel blessed in many ways.

Let Us Pray:

Our Father of Infinite Blessings, today, we take time to contemplate the ways in which we are blessed. Thank You for our Heavenly blessings and for our earthly blessings which sustain us and reveal Your majesty to us through Nature. We enter this Holy Moment to more fully experience gratitude for all of the excellent benefits of Your Generosity. Thank You God for the perfection of each gift and each blessing given at the ideal time and in Your perfect way. Lord we now look for opportunities to demonstrate our gratitude by blessing others, blessing the earth and living lives with a sense of joy, appreciation, gratitude and generosity that serves a world that works for everyone.

Thank You God!
So It Is!
Amen!
Selah!

"For I was hungry, and you gave me food to eat. I was thirsty, and you gave me drink. I was a stranger, and you took me in. I was naked, and you clothed me. I was sick, and you visited me. I was in prison, and you came to me."
— Matthew 25:35-36

"The King will answer them, 'Most certainly I tell you, because you did it to one of the least of these my brothers, you did it to me."
- Matthew 25:40

Self-Reflection Questions

Question 1: What do you recall about a time when you felt you had blessed another person?

_____

_____

_____

_____

_____

_____

Question 2: In what ways is your success related to blessing other people?

_____

_____

_____

_____

_____

_____

_____

My Thoughts

Harvesting a New Possibility

I let go of the past and
co-create my future with God.

"Behold, I will create new heavens and a new earth. The former things will not be remembered, nor will they come to mind."
– Isaiah 65:17

In this holy moment, consider your life regarding where you have been and where you are going. Do you feel that you are on the path to your highest good? Are you living in guilt, shame or regret because of something in your past, or do you feel you can't succeed because of past failures? If you harbor any of these or similar feelings, now is the time to let them go, forgive yourself and everyone in your past so that you can move forward into a bright future of love, fulfillment, and prosperity. Consider how you have grown from your experiences. Can you see how the hardships in years past have molded you into the stronger, more resilient individual you are today?

The future is a vast ocean of opportunity and possibility. Today ask God to chart your course, and set sail for your "new world" filled with peace, service, happiness, generosity and abundance.

Let Us Pray:

Our Father, through Whom all things are possible, I thank you for the life lessons my mistakes have taught me. I now realize that mistakes are a part of life, and personal experience can be an effective way to learn. Today I enjoy the wisdom rising from the ashes of my past. I understand that moving into the future of Divine Promise starts with taking a decisive first step today. Dear Lord, the Strength You Are gives me the courage to move confidently into the experience of my prayers fulfilled. Christ is the Way and Jesus is my Way-shower. Thank You, Jesus for transforming my relationship to the past and preparing me for the Harvest at hand. Alleluia! May God be glorified in my life! I see and feel the reality of my prayers and my purpose fulfilled! I am profoundly grateful.

Thank You God!
Selah!
Amen!

"Don't you say, 'There are yet four months until the harvest?' Behold, I tell you, lift up your eyes, and look at the fields, that they are white for harvest already."
- John 4:35 (WEB)

Self-Reflection Questions

Question 1: What would you love to see fulfilled in your life?

_____

_____

_____

_____

_____

_____

Question 2: What are you inspired to do today that would contribute to the answer to your prayers?

_____

_____

_____

_____

_____

_____

_____

My Thoughts

Today I Choose
Mental Images of Prosperity

I allow images of God's Will
for me to fill my mind.

"Remember me, O LORD, when you show favor to your people, come to my aid when you save them, that I may enjoy the prosperity of your chosen ones, that I may share in the joy of your nation and join your inheritance in giving praise."
– Psalms 106:4&5

I am immersed in the Energy of God's Wisdom and I allow God's Vision of my Highest Good to come forth as clear, attractive and compelling images, which call me forward into more abundant Life. I have a clear vision into which I live. I develop the habit of allowing images of prosperity to fill my mind. I do this by turning the camera of my attention from snapshots of lack, to landscapes of abundance. I engage my faculty of imagination in service to plenty and prosperity for everyone within my sphere of influence. What I see with my inner eye is more powerful than what appears to my physical eye. I have faith in God's nature of abundance and generosity. Today, I experience my consciousness of God within me as my only Source of supply. Christ within me is the Divine Power which restores the years the locusts have eaten and makes all things new. Christ lifts me up to see the unfolding possibilities of abundant prosperity.

Let Us Pray:

Thank You God for Your precious gifts of Spirit, especially Imagination, allowing for so many expressions of our gratitude. We thank You for our growing understanding of Spirit's transcendence as First Cause. Teach us, Father, to see You in every circumstance. Reveal Your image of every person we encounter or about whom we think. Remind us to let go of limiting, restrictive and destructive pictures and replace them with images of Divine Love, possibility, creativity, harmony and order. Thank You God for blessing us with the free will to choose, and the imagination to see what the naked eye cannot see. In this holy moment, we choose Your Vision of our Highest Good and the Highest Good of a world that works for everyone.

Thank You God!
So It Is!
Amen!

"You will be made rich in every way so that you can be generous on every occasion, and through us your generosity will result in thanksgiving to God. This service that you perform is not only supplying the needs of God's people but is also overflowing in many expressions of thanks to God."
– 2 Corinthians 9:11&12

Self-Reflection Questions

Question 1: What are the mental images of prosperity that inspire you to action?

_____

_____

_____

_____

_____

_____

Question 2: In what ways will you imagine prosperity today?

_____

_____

_____

_____

_____

_____

_____

My Thoughts

I Am Peaceful

My thoughts are in harmony with Peace.

"For the sake of my brothers and my friends, I will now say, 'May peace be within you.'"
- Psalm 122:8

I enjoy good health, peace of mind, and I am grateful for the overall wellbeing of the people in my life. I work to ensure that I live positively and bring peace wherever I go. I am healthy, strong and vibrant. When I notice that I am agitated or annoyed, I engage in a practice that reestablishes my positive attitude I find peace. Each day I remember that "Peace Begins with Me".

I notice what I feel and I observe the thoughts related to those feelings. Then I begin a process of choosing more healthy, life-giving thoughts which cause me to feel better and restore my energy. No matter what I face, I endeavor to be grateful. Since I orient myself with gratefulness, I often find joy. Even so, I am more peaceful, I stress less and relax more. I am healthier and happier than ever before. Today, I embrace peace and focus my thoughts on harmony, gratitude, and well-being.

Let Us Pray:

Our Father in heaven, Author of ultimate Peace, thank You! We thank You for peace! We are grateful for the Peace of Christ bestowed upon humanity. This Peace is available for the asking given the willingness to release the attitudes, beliefs and habits that inhibit, block or steal our peace. In this sacred moment, I surrender to the Holy Spirit and allow Christ-Love to surround me and hug me. I whisper to myself, "Thank God, Peace, Be Still!" May the peace that surpasses my common-hour understanding bring clarity, rejuvenation, insight and awareness that defy earth-bound reason, and outer appearances.

Thank You, God!
Selah!

"*Peace I leave with you; My peace I give to you; not as the world gives do I give to you. Do not let your heart be troubled, nor let it be fearful.*"
John 14:27

Self-Reflection Questions

Question 1: In what ways can you keep your thoughts in harmony with peace?

_____

_____

_____

_____

_____

_____

Question 2: What are the best ways for you to enhance the peace in your life?

_____

_____

_____

_____

_____

_____

_____

My Thoughts

I Forgive and I Am Forgiven Today

God's Love empowers me to forgive.

"For you, Lord, are good, and ready to forgive; Abundant in loving kindness to all those who call on you."
- Psalms 86:5

Today, during the time I choose to rest, and contemplate Love, I welcome opportunities to forgive and ask for forgiveness. I thank God for the life-saving, Soul cleansing power of forgiveness. When I practice forgiveness in my Inner Sanctuary, I become more receptive to the activity of the Holy Spirit in my encounters throughout my day.

Who can you forgive today? Is there a person who consistently annoys or offends you? Do you need to forgive this person or do you need to forgive yourself regarding your thoughts and behavior regarding her or him? Perhaps this moment is a perfect opportunity for you to learn how to love more completely and discover that transcendent Love is sufficient for forgiveness.

The Lord's Nature of Love empowers us to overcome the limitations of personality and conditioned thinking. In the conscious awareness of Almighty Love, we can restore, renew, and re-energize our ways of thinking, our relationships, and say Yes to the Lord's call to love one another.

Let us pray:

Yes, Lord, Thank You! within this blessed moment, I intend to forgive and to seek forgiveness. I welcome Your assistance, Lord! When I give my attention to you, I am more loving and happy. As my mistakes, debts and transgressions come to mind, I seek to forgive those same qualities I attribute to others. In so doing, I forgive myself. Thank You, God! Thank You, for the strength and the courage to apologize and make amends where possible. I am forgiven, as I forgive others. How perfect! I always know when I have genuinely forgiven another, because I feel forgiven.

Thank You for the Gift of Forgiveness!
Thank You God for loving me!
For Christ's Sake,
Amen!

"For if you forgive men their trespasses, your heavenly Father will also forgive you."
- Matthew 6:14

Self-Reflection Questions

Question 1: Clear your mind and ask, "Who do I need to forgive today?"

_____

_____

_____

_____

_____

_____

_____

Question 2: Who would you like to forgive you?

_____

_____

_____

_____

_____

_____

_____

_____

My Thoughts

In This Holy Moment
I Can Begin Again

Almighty Love empowers me to persevere.

"Create in me a clean heart, O God, And renew a right and steadfast spirit within me."
- Psalm 51:10 (AMP)

Today, regardless of our circumstances we can begin again. Can you believe that it is God's will for us to be the best that we can be? Even if all you can do is to be willing to believe that God's will for us is Good and only Good, you can move forward in that willingness into a fulfilling life. The Energy of God resides within you as a powerful Presence ready to be recognized and released into expression as the Spirit of your Being. Be still and know the Lord of your Being now - feel God's presence - breathe in the Holy Spirit - allow the Holy Spirit to relax your body and calm your mind. Awake to the Christ Presence within, which is your connection to the Infinite Universe. Thank You God for this Holy Moment of Peace!

Let Us Pray:

Dear Father, universally present, within and around me, Author of my every blessing; I thank You for all of the possibilities of my life from this moment on. Lord give me the ability to see Your Good in every circumstance of my life. Show me my oneness with You and my fellow human beings. Prepare humanity for an awakening of global proportion and prepare me for my role in it. I now renew my mind and purify my heart as my first steps in readying my consciousness for Your Expression. Father, equip me to see Your influence and presence in every person and circumstance that touches my life. Lord, I thirst for you, let me drink of Your Water which cleanses me and quenches my thirst forever. I now set the intention to open myself for the full expression of Your Presence within. Father, I seek to be a part of Your new heaven and to co-create with You and the rest of humanity, a new earth which fulfills Your plan and promise from the beginning. In this holy moment, I choose renewal, redemption and expanding capabilities. I am renewed! I am rejuvenated!

Thank You God!

Selah!

"...but whoever drinks the water I give him will never thirst. Indeed, the water I give him will become in him a spring of water welling up to eternal life."

– John 4:14

Self-Reflection Questions

Question 1: What is calling for renewal in your life?

_____

_____

_____

_____

_____

_____

Question 2: Imagine you are drinking the water of Christ; how do you feel as you drink?

_____

_____

_____

_____

_____

_____

My Thoughts

I Call on the Strength of the Lord

I am transformed; my weaknesses have become strengths.

"Trust ye in the LORD forever: for in the LORD JEHOVAH is everlasting strength."
- Isaiah 26:4 (KJV)

Today if you are facing a challenge or living in the fullness of Spirit's freedom, feel the Strength of the Lord propelling you forward. All of us make choices each day. Some we make unconsciously and then wonder why we are experiencing unpleasant circumstances. We consciously make other choices and we understand their effect on our experience. As you choose today, make your choices knowing that the Strength of the Lord is empowering you to be who God created you to be and to do what's yours to do. Have faith that you are functioning in full alignment with your highest Good. Today, be transformed according to the renewing of your mind and draw strength from Jesus' example in the Garden of Gethsemane. Then, whether your choices feel difficult or easy, surrender to God and declare, "Lord, not my will but Your Will be done."

Let Us Pray:

Thank You God for this day. I feel Your love for me and I am empowered to express the Christ Nature of my Being and do that which is mine to do... even the difficult and seemingly impossible. As I express Christ within me, I confidently speak and act because I am centered in the consciousness of Your Presence as an instrument of Love. I am Your loving, courageous and obedient creation dear Lord, and I intentionally align my will with Your Will. You are my strength, my confidence and my comfort. Today I triumphantly glorify my Father in Heaven and create the possibility of transformation for myself and others within my Sphere of Influence.

Praise God!
Selah!

"And I, if I be lifted up from the earth, I will draw all men unto me."
- John 12:32 (KJV)

Self-Reflection Questions

Question 1: How does God's Strength manifest in you?

_____

_____

_____

_____

_____

_____

_____

Question 2: How do your choices impact your sense of transformation?

_____

_____

_____

_____

_____

_____

_____

My Thoughts

Today I Intend to Be Steadfast in Love

I focus my attention on my intention to love.

"He will not be afraid of evil tidings; His heart is steadfast, trusting in the Lord."
- Psalm 112:7

I am endeavoring to live this day in Love. The Christ of my Being is teaching me focus, resilience and commitment. I stand in Love; I walk in Love and if I fall, as I attempt to move forward, I fall in Love. When I fall, I fall in Love with Immanuel: God-with-me. God is my Saving Grace, and I choose to be attentive to Love's Presence. No matter what happens, my fervent intention is to recognize the Holy Spirit speaking to me, speaking through me, guiding my steps and directing my actions. And when I am being guided into unfamiliar territory, requiring more than my experience has taught me, I let go of the familiar and let God, the I Am that I Am, move me forward in faith. My faith in God and my trust in Love are expanding and evolving.

Let us pray:

Dear Lord, consecrate my intention to be steadfast in Love. Thank You Lord for reminding me of Your Presence here and now. I choose to live in Christ and love You with my entire mind, with all of my heart, and with all of my strength. I rejoice in unexpected events and welcome the opportunity to grow in faith and the Truth of Being. Father, I am grateful for the assistance of the Holy Spirit, strengthening my resolve to stay focused on Love's possibilities. May my attention be unwaveringly on Love Almighty! I no longer fear bad news. I trust You Father. I rely on Your Loving Presence! Let Peace reside in me!

Thank You God!
So May It Be!
And So It Is!
Amen!

"Fear not, for I am with you; Be not dismayed, for I am your God. I will strengthen you, Yes, I will help you, I will uphold you with My righteous right hand."
- Isaiah 41:10

Self-Reflection Questions

Question 1: How do you imagine being in Love with God?

_____

_____

_____

_____

_____

_____

Question 2: What are some of the conditions that you have attached to Love?

_____

_____

_____

_____

_____

_____

My Thoughts

The Currency of Blessings Is Love

I keep my love circulating and creating blessings for others and for me.

"This is my commandment, that you love one another, even as I have loved you."
- John 15:12

As I endeavor to ascend in Love today, I ask, "How shall I serve God?" How will you serve God today, with good works, gifts to people in need, eloquent words, profound teachings? If what we do is not done in love, we will have accomplished nothing. God is Love; therefore, let us serve God today as though we were serving nutritious, life-giving sustenance to those we would bless. Woven into the fabric of our being is the need to love and to be loved. In this Holy Moment let's freely give love as thoughts of wellbeing, words of encouragement, comfort and peace or an acknowledging touch. I invite you to keep your abiding passion for well-being circulating through acts of kindness, healing prayers, and uplifting, Love-infused conversations. Be patient, understanding and energetically supportive to those who come into your thoughts and your presence today. Love and bless every one of whom you are conscious, even your enemies or those with whom you are at odds. Restore love to your relationships through forgiveness. Today let our first intention be to keep our desire for well-being and goodwill circulating by loving each other, even as God loves us.

Let Us Pray:

Dear God, You are Love Itself, allow me to experience a newly deepened relationship with You today. Lord, show me how to love my neighbor as I love myself and show me how to love myself as You love me, with pure Love freely given. My intention for the rest of this day Lord is to love with all of my heart, all of my mind and all of my soul. Give me the courage, the wisdom and the opportunity to love and to be loved today, Father. I am happiest when I am conscious of Love. Therefore I choose love at every decision point and I appreciate those who delight me, challenge me to grow in love or otherwise bring out the best in me. Thank You God for creating me in Your image as a loving Being capable of miraculous feats of Love.

I Thank You God!
It Is So!
Selah!

"And He said to them, "Render therefore to Caesar the things that are Caesar's, and to God the things that are God's."
- Luke 20:25

Self-Reflection Questions

Question 1: How do you keep love circulating in your life?

_____

_____

_____

_____

_____

_____

Question 2: How do you wish to be blessed at this moment?

_____

_____

_____

_____

_____

_____

_____

My Thoughts

Opportunities for Inspired Action

I am grateful for this day!

"This is the day the Lord has made; We will rejoice and be glad in it."
- Psalm 118:24

Thank God for this day! This day contains opportunities for prayerful reflection, opportunities for inspired action and the opportunity for new experiences — not those found in my personal history, but emerging from it as the fulfilling of Universal Law.

It is good to be alive and awake to Love's Presence in my life and to God's presence in the lives of everyone within my sphere of influence, directly or indirectly. I am blessed by the primary Presence of Christ in me and the residual impact of Christ-inspired action in the world.

Let us thank God for the circumscribing Love-inspired activities, which serve the nurturing of humanity and fill this day with joy, transformation, celebration and gladness. As we mindfully live this day, we fulfill our individual and collective purpose for the benefit of humanity.

Let Us Pray:

How good it is to live this day guided by Divine purpose replete with inspired action! Today, I live my mission as best I can with the intention of following Christ's guidance in the expression of the I AM that I Am. I thank God, the Source and Fountain from Which flows every good and perfect gift. Thank You Jesus, Champion of the Best, always making yesterday's good Better. Each day in every way, I am better and better at being the best I can be in the eternal now moment. Thank God, Love Almighty! What action is mine to take in the expression of my purpose today? I hear; I obey!

Thank You, God!

Amen!

"Do you not believe that I am in the Father, and the Father in Me? The words that I speak to you I do not speak on My own authority; but the Father who dwells in Me does the works."
- John 14:10

Self-Reflection Questions

Question 1: Who do you know yourself to be in this now moment?

_____

_____

_____

_____

_____

_____

Question 2: How do you intend to celebrate Life today?

_____

_____

_____

_____

_____

_____

My Thoughts

Peace Begins with Me

The peace present in me
blesses the world.

"Pray for the peace of Jerusalem. Those who love you will prosper." - Psalms 122:6

Let today be a day we pray for each other, everyone in our circle of friends and family and every one of whom we can possibly think. You and I can follow the literal, scriptural guidance of Psalms 122:6, as we pray for the city of Jerusalem and for peace throughout the region of the Middle East. Let us thank God that the unifying order we hold in our heart is manifested throughout the world, in our communities, in our family, in the lives of our friends and in the awareness of those we may characterize as enemies or adversaries.

The Metaphysical Bible Dictionary defines Biblical Jerusalem as the habitation of peace and the abode of prosperity. In us it is the abiding consciousness of spiritual calm, which is centered in the nerve complex just in back of the heart. Therefore, in our prayers today let us place our focus on the area surrounding and including our heart and seek the experience of peace which goes beyond our intellectual understanding.

Let Us Pray:

Dear Lord, let there be peace on earth and let it begin with me! As I focus my attention on my heart, I feel it beating in a constant, reliable rhythm. I appreciate my heart and its faithful, life-sustaining activity. I bless my heart and I am thankful for the peace of mind its unceasing functioning gives me. As I experience the peace of my heart, I now project that peace and the Peace of God onto my family, friends and all in my immediate community. As the images and the feelings of communal harmony grow stronger, I extend my consciousness of peace into the world at large. I Thank You God for Your peace on earth and thank You for its presence in me.

"And the peace of God, which surpasses all understanding, will guard your hearts and minds through Christ Jesus."
- Philippians 4:7 (NJKV)

Self-Reflection Questions

Question 1: Where are you when you feel most peaceful?

_____

_____

_____

_____

_____

_____

Question 2: When you feel peaceful, what are some of your most peaceful thoughts?

_____

_____

_____

_____

_____

_____

_____

My Thoughts

I Value Humility

I am humble, I am responsible, the Earth is my inheritance.

"A man's pride brings him low, But one of lowly spirit gains honor." - Proverbs 29:23

"But the humble shall inherit the land, And shall delight themselves in the abundance of peace."
- Psalms 37:11

When I think about the people I admire, those who are most exceptional are the ones who exhibit excellence and humility. For me, being humble allows me to demonstrate that I am human and vulnerable. My missteps remind me of my fallibility. My humility ensures I can learn from my mistakes and move on.

To me, to be humble means to behave in a modest and unpretentious way. I avoid being overly prideful or arrogant. I feel my arrogance separating me from the truth about myself and others. My humility helps me to put things into proper perspective.

Because I believe that each human being is unique and essential, my humility remains steady whether I am dealing with a supervisor, someone I supervise, a close friend, a family member or a child.

Today, I reflect on my unique blending of self-esteem and humility. I am comfortably humble before God and my fellow human beings. My life is rewarding and fulfilling. I am humbly grateful!

Let Us Pray:

Dear Lord, thank You for the times You remind me to be humble. When I have felt humiliation, I realize that I have had an opportunity to temper my pride and let go of arrogant self-centeredness. When I consider myself humble, I wait for Your confirmation in my spirit; I release any pride in my humility. I thank you God for the peace of humility and Your Love for me. I am blessed beyond measure and I am grateful!

Amen!

"Blessed are the meek, for they shall inherit the earth."
- Matthew 5:5

Self-Reflection Questions

Question 1: In what ways do you feel good about yourself and remain healthily humble?

_____

_____

_____

_____

_____

_____

Question 2: What does healthy self-esteem mean to you?

_____

_____

_____

_____

_____

_____

_____

My Thoughts

Reflect and Recommit to Life

I am renewed in Spirit and realigned with God.

"Create in me a clean heart, O God. Renew a right spirit within me." - Psalms 51:10

Let us take time today to reflect on who we have been, who we are now being and who God created us to be. Are you the best person that you would like to be now? Are there other ways of being that would help you feel better about yourself? Are you disappointed with your current circumstances? Are there ways of behaving that would contribute more harmony to your family or workplace? If the answer is yes, are you willing to explore new ways of thinking and doing? Once you recognize that something is amiss, choose new thoughts through renunciation and forgiveness. Let go of ineffective thought patterns and shift your perception of the present moment. You can experience renewed energy for healing and accomplishment and success in all of your endeavors. By directing your attention to your inner Christ Power of Love, you can experience new meanings, expanded awareness, and life-changing downloads of Truth that free you from bondage states of mind. The abundance and sense of well-being that you thought were lost are found and your life is set on a new trajectory. Let's resolve to remember: with God all things are possible!

Let Us Pray:

Thank You God for this day of reflection, repentance and renewal! I thank God for reminding me that the Holy Spirit is always present and accessible. Christ accepts me just as I am. When I acknowledge that I am out of alignment with Your Will and Your guidance, Lord, I renounce the negative thinking and actions which have led me to the experiences which seemed devoid of Your Presence. Enhance Your Power in me to discern the difference between Truth and error. I have now awakened to Truth and I am returning Home to You, Father. I feel the renewal of my mind, I think the thoughts which You have placed in Divine Mind and I make them my own. I repudiate my fear of sickness and disease and allow the perfect working of the Holy Spirit to restore my body to health and fitness. I abandon my belief in scarcity and insufficiency, and I replace it with the expression of Your indwelling Presence of prosperity and abundance. All is well in my life according to Your will and Your promise, through Christ Jesus. I recommit to living a God-Centered Life!

Thank You God!
So It Is!
Amen!

"And be not conformed to this world: but be ye transformed by the renewing of your mind, that ye may prove what is that good, and acceptable, and perfect, will of God."
- Romans 12:2 (KJV)

Self-Reflection Questions

Question 1: What thought patterns would you like to change?

_____

_____

_____

_____

_____

_____

Question 2: Which new thought pattern, will you assume to experience better conditions in your life?

_____

_____

_____

_____

_____

_____

_____

My Thoughts

Spiritual Peace

Today I choose to enter into the consciousness of Spiritual Peace.

"Rejoice greatly, daughter of Zion! Shout, daughter of Jerusalem! Behold, your king comes to you! He is righteous, and having salvation; Lowly, and riding on a donkey, Even on a colt, the foal of a donkey."
- Zechariah 9:9

Today, let us emulate Jesus by finding Peace in our "I AM" consciousness. We are being prepared for purification and ascension into a higher state of being. This is only possible with the crossing out of limiting thoughts and habits of personality which tend to edge God out of our conscious thinking and awareness. Charles Fillmore said, "When the I AM takes charge of the body a new order of things is inaugurated." This state of consciousness is characterized by sustainable vitality, high ideals and freedom from lower-frequency, influences. We begin to function with the license of one who comes in the name of the Lord when we surrender to the I AM that I Am.

Let Us Pray:

Dear Father in heaven, I thank you for guiding me to a raised consciousness of peace, spiritual power, spiritual poise and new confidence in Your Abiding Presence in my life and affairs. I elevate the I AM Presence that I am, to a place of dominion in my life. I Am, then, master of my ego. I release my ego from a position of control, and I entertain thoughts that are in alignment with Your Nature, Father. You are the "I AM" in me as Lord of my life. Just as You raised up Jesus, raise my thoughts, my speaking and my behavior to new levels of effectiveness and Truth. May Your blessing me be a blessing to all within my sphere of influence. Father, raise my self-awareness to the Truth I AM, teach me the Peace of Christ. I am made whole and complete!

Thank You God!
All Is Well!
Amen!

"Don't be afraid, daughter of Zion. Behold, your King comes, sitting on a donkey's colt."
- John 12:15

Self-Reflection Questions

Question 1: Why is your ego becoming more obedient to Christ in you?

_____

_____

_____

_____

_____

_____

Question 2: When you utter the words, "I AM", how conscious are you of the words that come next?

_____

_____

_____

_____

_____

_____

_____

My Thoughts

A Peaceful Mind Guides My Steps

I release the world's chaos
and embrace Love's Peace.

"Thou wilt keep him in perfect peace, whose mind is stayed on Thee: because he trusteth in Thee."
- Isaiah 26:3 KJV

I have faith in the power of PEACE. A peaceful mind paves the path that lies before me. Everything becomes easier when I calm my thoughts and quiet my mind. I trust in the peace of God which is more than understanding. I value the peace that comes from faith.

I endeavor to think only the best, to calmly work for the best, and to only expect the best; I find peacefulness and satisfaction in my endeavors. I feel at ease when I know I am contributing as much as I can. Sometimes I succeed in the short run. Sometimes the outcomes fall short of what I hope, but I know that my efforts are still worthwhile and I keep my attention focused on the wisdom of Love's Guidance.

I let go of worries, I breathe deeply, and I focus on the positive. When I experience so-called challenges, disappointments or failures, I refrain from labeling them or calling them 'bad'. I let go of disquieting judgments, and I imagine as many preferable outcomes as I can. I have faith that 'all is well'!

I practice forgiving myself and others and I experience the freedom of release. When I am angry, resentful or blaming, I take responsibility for my power to choose Love's peace instead of giving into the poison of bigotry, hatred or violence.

Let Us Pray:

Dear Lord, Why, am I strong enough to maintain my peace of mind? I trust Your Love and Forgiveness to bring me peace in my attempts to quiet my mind and cool my emotions. I thank You Lord, for reminding me of those times You lifted me out of difficult situations. Gratefulness and mindfulness bless my actions and my results. Help me focus on the present moment. I decline to dwell on the past or fear the future. In this Holy Moment, I clear my mind. I make room for peaceful thoughts and I await Your guidance.

Father, I am grateful for the benefits of maintaining a peaceful mind and a heart of peace.

Thank You,
I am in Peace!
Amen!

"Now may the Lord of peace Himself continually grant you peace in every circumstance. The Lord be with you all!" -
2 Thessalonians 3:16 (NASB)

Self-Reflection Questions

Question 1: What do you do to create space in your mind for peaceful thoughts?

_____

_____

_____

_____

_____

_____

Question 2: How is peace showing up in your experience?

_____

_____

_____

_____

_____

_____

_____

My Thoughts

God's Grace Is My Assurance of Peace

I am forgiven as I forgive; then I know Peace.

"Forgive us our debts, as we also forgive our debtors."
- Matthew 6:12

Most of us experience times when we wish there were more peace in our life. Our sense of disquiet could be due to discord in our home or workplace. It could be due to our private worries which we choose not to share with anyone. Or it may be no more than what we consider the normal stresses of everyday life, working, playing, and wondering "What's It All About." In times like these it is comforting to remember that God's Grace is sufficient. Let us take a few moments, regularly, in good times and bad, to choose to stop, take a deep breath and let go of our thoughts and feelings, and experience God's Present Grace. Affirm, "Through the Grace of God I am forgiven, healed and comforted with peace of mind." – (Paraphrased from Charles Fillmore's Keep A True Lent, "The Grace of God" page 168.

Let Us Pray:

Dear God, Sweet Holy Spirit, I surrender to Your Grace and accept Your Peace. I let go of the vexations of my spirit, I calm the restlessness in my mind and I allow the peaceful understanding of the power of Your Presence within me to sink into my knowing and being. I love You God! You Love me with the pure unconditional Love which empowers me to forgive others and myself. I choose Love over revenge, I choose peace over violence. I am grateful for the grace of free will, I accept Christ and follow the teaching of Jesus. Thank You God! I surrender the details of my life to Love's Wisdom. I prefer peace! I want forgiveness! I desire the Love of Jesus Christ, unconditional, freely given to friend and foe. I am at peace!

Thank You, God! Thank You, God! Thank You, God! Selah!

"He has said to me, "My grace is sufficient for you, for my power is made perfect in weakness." Most gladly therefore I will rather glory in my weaknesses, that the power of Christ may rest on me."
- 2 Corinthians 12:9

Self-Reflection Questions

Question 1: What is your experience of God's Peace at this moment?

_____

_____

_____

_____

_____

_____

_____

Question 2: In what way is God's Grace sufficient for you?

_____

_____

_____

_____

_____

_____

_____

My Thoughts

Why Am I Loved So Deeply?

I love from the depths of my being.

"Beloved, let us love one another, for love is of God; and everyone who loves is born of God, and knows God."
- 1 John 4:7

Recently, I became aware that I often ask disempowering questions, questions which are born in assumptions that are often antithetical to what I say I believe. For example, "Why can't I find an honest mechanic?" This type of 'why' question creates negative energy in my spirit. Even if I believe that the underlying assumption isn't always correct, I do not want to live my life as though it were true. Disempowering, implicit questions, which we rarely pause to question, create a lot of the cynicism and prejudice in the world. I was blessed by Noah St. John's book, Great Little Book of Afformations. The premise of the book is that we can plumb the depths of spiritual truth by asking empowering 'Why' questions that lead to pleasantly surprising love, healing, or harmony. I have had confirming experiences of love, especially God's Love, when I persistently ask, "Why Am I Loved so deeply?" My intention is that you experience God's Love anew as we pray together today.

Let Us Pray:

Dear Lord, why am I loved so deeply? I am not looking for one answer, Lord, I am looking for evidence of Love in my life. Why is there always a reassuring thought or comforting word available to me in my time of doubt or sadness? Why do I always know that You connect with me in my mind or You will get my attention through interactions with other people or the confluence of seemingly random events which help me realize a transcendent Truth? Why is Your Love within me more powerful than anything I see in the 'world'? Thank You God for loving me and caring for me so that Your Will is accomplished in me, through me and even as me. Dearest Lord, You are my hope, my assurance and my confidence in every situation. Why do You always bless my conditions, my encounters and all of my relationships? I revel in the blessings of Your Love. Why do You love me Lord? I cannot count the ways, I just accept the peace, the sense of well-being and the comfort I feel all are evidence of Your implicit Love.

Thank You God! I Rejoice in Your Love! Selah! Amen!

"But God, being rich in mercy, for his great love with which he loved us, even when we were dead through our trespasses, made us alive together with Christ (by grace you have been saved),"
- Ephesians 2:4-5 (WEB)

Self-Reflection Questions

Question 1: What is your most compelling, generative why question?

_____

_____

_____

_____

_____

_____

Question 2: What new ideas come to mind as you contemplate today's reading?

_____

_____

_____

_____

_____

_____

_____

My Thoughts

A Message from Immanuel:
What Is Mine to Know Today?

I sought, I asked, I found,
and now I receive.

"Ask, and it will be given you. Seek, and you will find. Knock, and it will be opened for you."
- Matthew 7:7

Dear Immanuel, thank You for this day! What is mine to know?

Dear One, I AM Immanuel, God-with-you. This is the most important day of your life. It is the only day that matters now. Live this day as if you were born this morning and will go to a higher plane of existence when you ease into sleep tonight. This day is your Life. Today, you can be as you most desire to be. Bless your soul by surrendering to My Presence as your new identity. Rejoice and be glad today. I have chosen this moment to have an out-of-body experience with you, so that I might speak to you in a manner that you can always recognize as My connection with you. Learn to Perceive My Wisdom, My Revelation, and My Inspiration. Let Me inspire you to Act. This moment is forever with you; hold it in the heart of your consciousness. I am with you always.

My Kingdom is in the process of coming through you now. I AM, at this moment speaking to you as if you and

I are separated, but in Truth, we are One Being, One Power, One Love, expressing on multiple planes. Be still! Be quiet! Know I AM God; I AM, That, I Am in the stillness of your soul. Feel the longing of your heart and the discontent in your soul, and choose what you long to be. Now recognize that I AM WHO; I AM is you Born Again!

Now dear One, Pray and meditate on the following scriptures:

[14] God said to Moses, "I AM WHO I AM," and he said, "You shall tell the children of Israel this: 'I AM has sent me to you." – Exodus 3:14

"Jesus said to him, "I am the way, the truth, and the life. No one comes to the Father, except through me." - John 14:6

"Whatever you will ask in my name, that will I do, that the Father may be glorified in the Son."
- John 14:13

Self-Reflection Questions

Question 1: What are you asking now?

_____

_____

_____

_____

_____

_____

Question 2: What you have asked is now given; what does it feel like to receive it?

_____

_____

_____

_____

_____

_____

_____

My Thoughts

Creating a Sabbath Moment

Today I experience peace
and clarity through meditation.

"My mouth shall speak of wisdom; and the meditation of my heart shall be of understanding."
- Psalms 49:3

Today I extend my time with the Lord in prayer and meditation. I surrender the shallow thinking of my brain to the peaceful awareness of Mind. I sit quietly, I become comfortable and gently place my attention on my breathing and let go of my conscious thinking. If thoughts enter my mind, I let them pass through and return my attention to my breath. I am aware of the filling of my lungs as I inhale. I consciously notice my inhalation before releasing it in a deliciously relaxing exhalation. I relax, I let go and dissolve the tension and stress in my body and I stop the restless activity of my intellect. Relaxed and peaceful, I spend time with the Lord experiencing Truth; my Oneness with my Creator.

Let Us Pray:

Our Father in heaven, we are resting, and uplifted in Your Presence. We thank You for Your Peace which surpasses our understanding. We rest in the quiet activity of Your healing, renewing and refreshing Spirit. In the silence of our physical rest, we are immersed in

Your Love and Knowing. We come to You in this holy moment with no agenda, except to experience the Silence of Your Being. We consciously enter Your presence with thanksgiving and we rest in the experience of Your Love which rises above all earthly concerns; we are renewed and inspired. Receptive to Your Vision and Your Revelations, we open our inner eyes and incline our ears to Your Still Small Voice.

Thank You God!
We Are Refreshed!
All Is Well!
So It is!
Amen!

"Come unto me, all ye that labor and are heavy laden, and I will give you rest."
- *Matthew 11:28 KJV*

Self-Reflection Questions

Question 1: How would you communicate your experience of the Peace of God that is beyond ordinary understanding! *(Remember, there are many forms of verbal and non-verbal communication)*

_____

_____

_____

_____

_____

_____

_____

Question 2: What can you write about your relationship to peace, divine and temporal?

_____

_____

_____

_____

_____

_____

_____

My Thoughts

About the Author

Charles W. Thomas, Jr. spent the first half of his life pursuing the belief that reality consisted of what can be measured, manipulated and used for practical purposes. He has spent the last 18 years studying spirituality with an emphasis on prayer and  forgiveness as spiritual keys. He is now devoting his life to understanding the subjective side of Life, that is, nurturing the concept that this understanding may be significant in determining for ourselves what comprises reality.

Charles has written A Month of Sundays as a tool for people who, like himself, are on a path of spiritual discovery. He has found that engaging in daily prayer and devotion makes a noticeable difference in one's outlook on life, and that it contributes wondrously to peace of mind. His prayer for this book, A Month of Sundays, is that it become a gentle companion for Truth-seekers who desire a more intimate relationship with the Spirit-of-Love residing within.

In his roles as Lay Minister of the Detroit Unity Temple Forgiveness Ministry and as a Life Mastery Consultant, certified by Mary Morrissey's Life Mastery Institute, Charles has experienced the effectiveness of persistent action, spaced repetition and the cultivation of the 'Witness-Self' — that part of us that is aware of our awareness. The dynamic product of all this: A Month of Sundays is the first book in a series of books entitled New Day – New Manna, Daily Sustenance for Being. This series of books is designed to help Truth-seekers explore the landscape of their inner-consciousness, to discover the often-hidden aspects of their sense of identity, and to document their experiences for future reflection and harvesting.

Made in the USA
Lexington, KY
29 November 2019